DONKEY

2

When I was a little boy, we lived in some upstairs rooms. My friends all lived far away. I had to play on my own. I would see how many stairs I could jump at one go or how many flies I could swat in an hour. I dressed up and pretended to be all kinds of things.

But one summer I got bored. I didn't want to
play by myself anymore. I was lonely.

I spent all my time standing on our balcony.
From there, I could look down on the busy street
below us. The whole street was a market, full of
people buying and selling things. Donkeys were
tethered to many of the fruit and vegetable carts.
I watched those donkeys for hours and hours,
dreaming that one day I might own one.

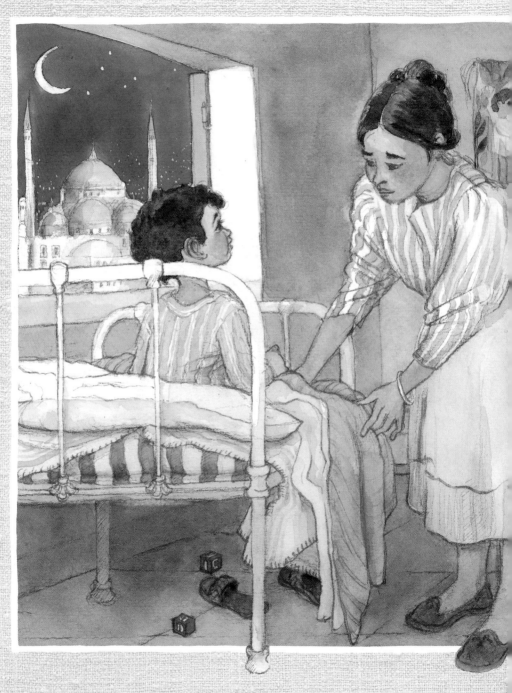

My birthday was only a few weeks away.
"Mom," I said. "Do you know what I'd really like for my birthday? A donkey!"

For a while, she was too surprised to speak. Then she said, ''Impossible! You can't have one.''

I wanted to know why not.

She said we couldn't afford to buy one.

I said I'd save up all my money and do lots of extra jobs to help pay for it.

She said we wouldn't have enough food to feed it.

I said I'd share all my meals with it.

She said we had nowhere to keep it.

I said I'd keep it in my bedroom.

She said nothing to that and I thought I'd won. But a while later she raised her voice and said, "The whole idea's quite ridiculous! Have you forgotten we live on the third floor? Donkeys can't climb stairs."

I was heartbroken. I didn't know that donkeys couldn't climb stairs. As long as we had stairs, I would never have a donkey.

One afternoon, I was watching from our balcony. I saw something interesting. A donkey was wandering about the street on its own. It stopped here and there to pick up scraps of vegetables on the road. No one seemed to take any notice of it.

I half flew down the stairs. On the street, I walked up to the donkey. I went slowly, so no one could see what I was up to.

I scratched the donkey's flat forehead. It looked at me as though I were an old friend. I found a few good cabbage leaves in the gutter and held one close to its mouth. It crunched greedily and stepped toward me for more. I held another leaf just out of its reach. This way, I was able to lead the donkey through the crowds to our stairs.

I turned it around to face the stairs. "If only I could teach it to climb stairs," I thought.

I decided to get behind it and try to push it up. I put my hands on its rump. Before I could start pushing, it kicked with both its back legs and quickly went up the stairs. I ran behind it. I couldn't believe my eyes.

I caught its tail and stopped it by putting my
left leg against the rail. Then I grabbed its mane and
let it slowly drag me to just outside our door.

With one hand, I took out my key and opened
the door. The donkey followed me inside. I felt
happier than I'd ever felt before. I kissed the donkey
all over its soft black nose. I hugged its neck many
times. Then I led it into my bedroom.

Mom was out shopping that afternoon. When I heard her turning the key in the lock, I ran to her.

"Mom! Mom!" I shouted. "I've got a surprise for you."

She pushed me out of the way and put down her heavy shopping baskets. Then she sat down. It was a hot day and she was tired out.

"Run away and play," she told me. "Can't you see I'm tired?"

"But, Mom, I've got a terrific surprise for you," I said. "Close your eyes and don't open them until I say. Oh, come on, Mom, please!"

She closed her eyes with a tired groan.

I went into the bedroom and quickly pulled the donkey out behind me. I put it right in front of Mom. Their two noses were almost touching.

"Ready!" I said.

Mom opened her eyes.

For a few seconds, the donkey and Mom just stared at each other. Then Mom began to scream and the donkey began to bray. The noise was deafening.

"He's my donkey," I said, when the noise had died down a little.

"Get that filthy animal out of my house!" she yelled.

"But, Mom, I found him," I said. "And he's very smart — he can climb stairs without any help!"

"I don't care what he can do — he's going right now!" she ordered.

She found an old rope and tied it around the donkey's neck. With the carpet-beater in her hand, she chased us down the stairs.

As soon as we were out on the street, an old man came running.

"Hey! That's my donkey!" he shouted at my mother.

"Well, you're lucky," she told him. "My son found it wandering and he looked after it for you."

"You her son?" he asked me. I nodded.

"Then you're a very good boy," he said. He took a small silver coin from his pocket and pressed it into my hand.

After that, I cried on and off for weeks. We never talked about that day again. But I've never stopped loving donkeys. Even today, if I meet one, I scratch its forehead. Then I hug its neck and — if there's no one watching — I kiss it.